BIBLE FACTS

CANDLE
BOOKS

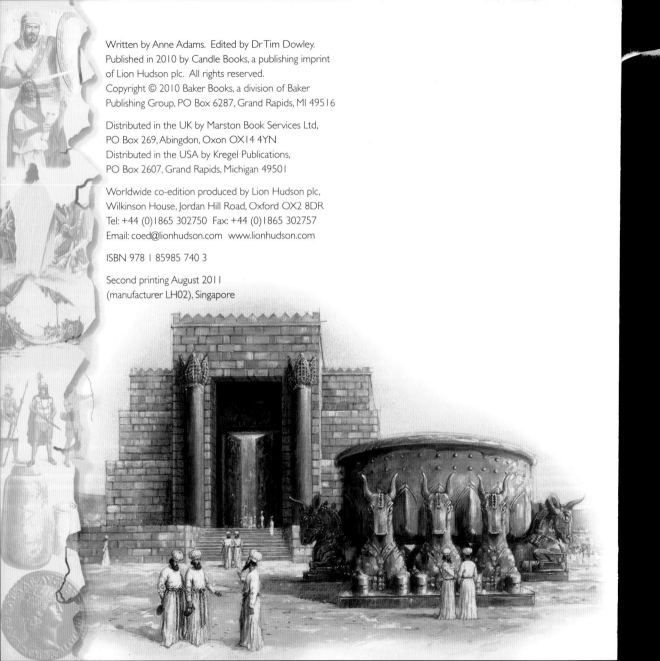

Written by Anne Adams. Edited by Dr Tim Dowley.
Published in 2010 by Candle Books, a publishing imprint
of Lion Hudson plc. All rights reserved.
Copyright © 2010 Baker Books, a division of Baker
Publishing Group, PO Box 6287, Grand Rapids, MI 49516

Distributed in the UK by Marston Book Services Ltd,
PO Box 269, Abingdon, Oxon OX14 4YN
Distributed in the USA by Kregel Publications,
PO Box 2607, Grand Rapids, Michigan 49501

Worldwide co-edition produced by Lion Hudson plc,
Wilkinson House, Jordan Hill Road, Oxford OX2 8DR
Tel: +44 (0)1865 302750 Fax: +44 (0)1865 302757
Email: coed@lionhudson.com www.lionhudson.com

ISBN 978 1 85985 740 3

Second printing August 2011
(manufacturer LH02), Singapore

Contents

The women's section of a tent.

The Tent-maker

Tents were used by nomads who moved around frequently in search of food and water for their animals. They were easy to take down and carry. Early Israelites, such as Abraham, used tents. So did desert-dwellers such as the Nabateans and the Bedouin (*Genesis 13:18*).

A Bedouin tent today.

How to build a tent

Parts needed	quantity
Woven goats' hair	10
Wooden toggles	20
Wooden tent-poles	6–9
Ropes	20
Stakes	20

How a tent was constructed.

Setting up the tent

1. Sew together woven goats'-hair pieces to make one large sheet.
2. Pound the poles into the ground.
3. Spread the goats'-hair covering over the poles.
4. Tie the covering down with ropes attached to pegs driven into the ground.

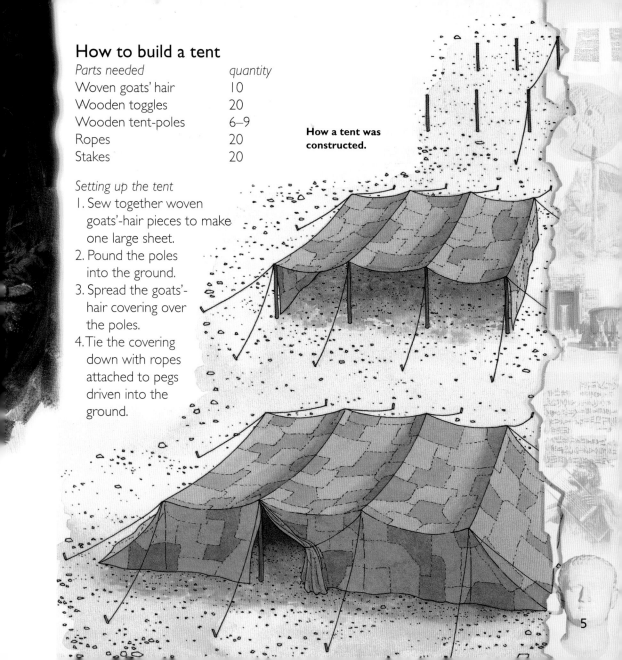

5

The earliest tent-makers made tents from leather. Later, they used goats' or camel hair. Goats' hair could be woven into a very strong material. It was naturally waterproof and tough enough to withstand strong desert winds and the scorching sun.

More about tents

- While the average family tent had nine poles, important families had more.
- Rich families had several tents. There were separate tents for women, children and servants. The main tent was in the middle.
- Tent doors were left open to welcome visitors.
- When tents were worn or torn, they could be patched with new pieces of skin or woven hair.
- The very best goats' hair, called *cilicium*, came from the Roman province of Cilicia. Paul learned the craft of tent-making in his hometown of Tarsus, in Cilicia (modern Turkey).

The Tabernacle in the wilderness was a tent temple (Exodus 26:7). This cut-away illustration shows inside the tent. Do you know what the golden object is?

A Bedouin tent in the Judean desert.

Tent-makers of Bible times.
Notice their sharp knives and
strong needles.

Who lived in tents?

1. Fathers of the Jewish nation such as Abraham, Isaac, Jacob and Joseph (*Genesis 18:1*).
2. Desert nomad tribes such as the Bedouin and Nabateans.
3. The Israelites in the wilderness (*Exodus 16:16*).
4. Soldiers in army encampments and warriors such as David (*2 Kings 7:7; 1 Samuel 17:54*).
5. Craftsmen such as carpenters and masons, working on projects away from home.
6. Herdsmen.

Bible Nugget

When Paul went on his missionary journeys, he was able to make money by working as a tent-maker – the trade he learned as a boy.
Acts 18:3

A bedouin family around their tent.

Houses

Most homes were made of rough stone, or mud and straw bricks. Tar was used for mortar (*Genesis 11:3*).

In ordinary houses, the courtyard doubled as a kitchen and led indoors to a living room. The flat roof was ideal for drying clothes, figs and grapes and also good for sleeping, eating and praying. Small, high windows kept the house cool in summer, warm in winter. Wall hollows were used to store pots. The walls were whitewashed.

In most homes, the animals stayed in part of the house at night.

Doors were low, and adults had to stoop to enter. Most didn't have locks, but bolts or iron bars.

A cutaway illustration of a house in Bible times.

Inside a house of Bible times. Notice the pots and baskets used for storage.

11

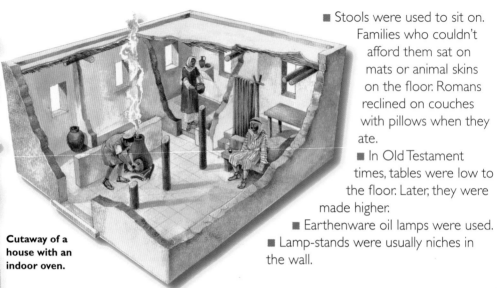

■ Stools were used to sit on. Families who couldn't afford them sat on mats or animal skins on the floor. Romans reclined on couches with pillows when they ate.

■ In Old Testament times, tables were low to the floor. Later, they were made higher.

■ Earthenware oil lamps were used.

■ Lamp-stands were usually niches in the wall.

Cutaway of a house with an indoor oven.

Furniture for most people was very simple:

■ Beds were usually mats that were rolled up during the day. Sometimes people slept on a raised platform inside the house. Kings and the very rich slept on bronze, iron or elaborate wooden beds.

Cutaway of a house with a "booth", or shelter, on the roof.

An Eastern house with a yard
for the animals to graze.
Notice the outdoor oven.

13

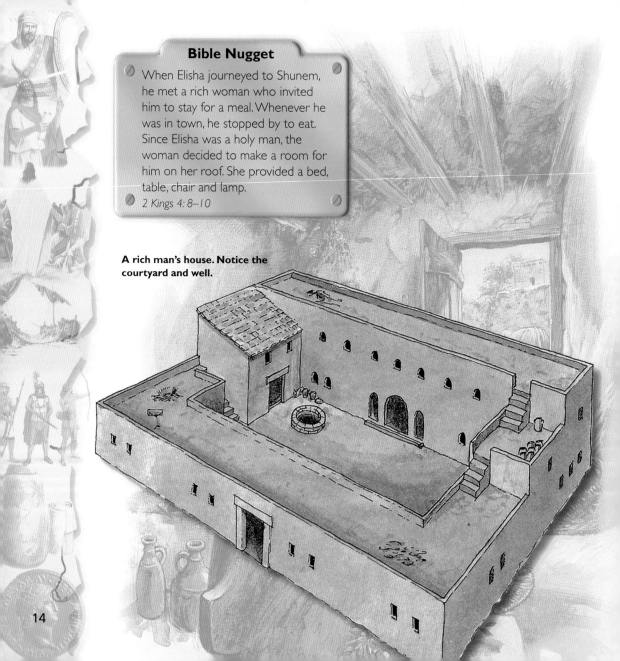

Bible Nugget

When Elisha journeyed to Shunem, he met a rich woman who invited him to stay for a meal. Whenever he was in town, he stopped by to eat. Since Elisha was a holy man, the woman decided to make a room for him on her roof. She provided a bed, table, chair and lamp.

2 Kings 4: 8–10

A rich man's house. Notice the courtyard and well.

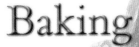

Baking

Baking bread was an important task done mostly by women or slaves. Wheat made the most tasty and nutritious bread, but those who couldn't afford it used barley.

A bread oven of Bible times.

In the earliest days, grain was pounded with a stone mortar and pestle (*Proverbs 27:22*). Coarse bits, not yet flour, were used to make the dough.

Later, a hand mill (*Exodus 11:5*) was used to produce flour. Grain was ground between two rough millstones. A rotary mill was used even later.

A hand mill for grinding grain.

15

Bread was baked fresh every few days, since it quickly turned stale.

In more modern times, cities and larger villages had a public baker. Women prepared the dough, then brought it to town to be baked in larger, public ovens. The baker's boy returned the bread to its owners, carrying some of the loaves on his head.

Public bakers were so important in Jerusalem that a road was called "Baker's Street" (*Jeremiah 37:21*).

Royal bakers made breads or cakes just for the royal household (*Genesis 40:5*).

A clay oven for baking bread.

Two women grind grain. In the background is a jar oven.

Recipe for bread

1. Grind coarse grain or flour, preferably wheat or barley with water.
2. Salt a little fermented dough saved from the previous day.
3. Mix the above ingredients.
4. Knead the mixture in a wooden bowl or kneading trough to form a pliable dough. It will be sticky.
5. Let the dough rise for several hours.
6. Shape into flat loaves and bake.

Types of oven

- *Bowl oven*: the simplest and one of the most ancient. The bowl was made of clay and turned upside down on small stones. Hot, dry dung was heaped under it.
- *Jar oven*: large stone or copper jars were half-filled with hot pebbles, heated wood or grass. When the jar was hot, the top was closed and the dough was placed on top to bake.
- *Pit oven*: this clay oven was built partly below ground and partly above. The fire was made inside.
- *Barrel oven*: this type was especially popular in Palestine and Syria. A barrel-shaped hole in the ground was plastered with clay and heated with dung and straw.

17

Desserts

- Cakes were sweetened with honey, or mint or cinnamon were added.
- Honey doughnuts were cut into animal shapes and deep-fried in olive oil.
- Locust biscuits were made with ground, sun-dried locusts, honey and wheat flour.

Baking bread over a bowl oven.

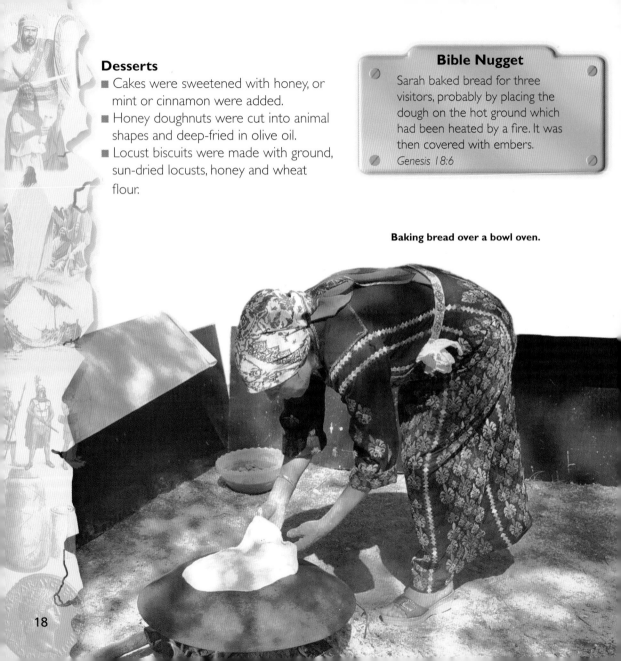

Meals

There were usually two meals a day. Breakfast was light, consisting of bread, dried fruit and cheese. It was usually eaten on the way to the fields or workplace.

Workers sometimes took a "packed lunch" with them to the fields. A typical lunch was two small hollowed-out loaves of bread filled with olives and cheese.

Men enjoy a feast seated on cushions.

The main meal was eaten with the family at the end of the working day. The Egyptians ate their main meal at noon rather than at the end of the day (*Genesis 43:16*).

A Jewish family celebrate the festival of Passover.

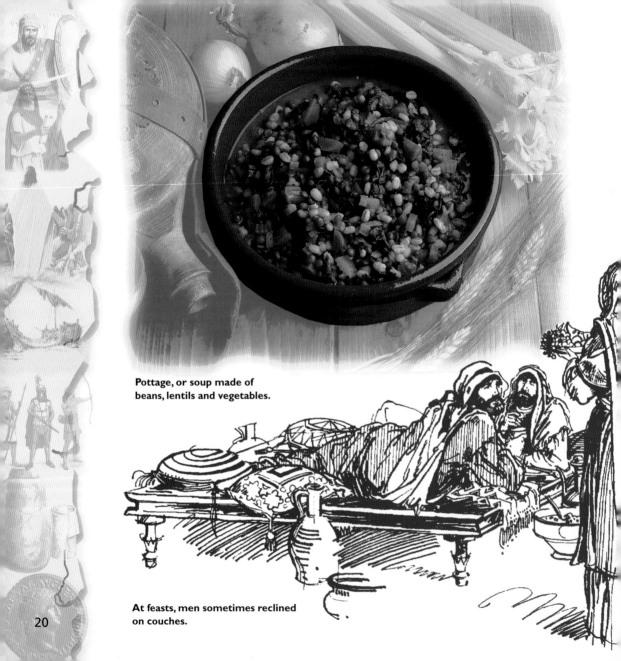

Pottage, or soup made of
beans, lentils and vegetables.

At feasts, men sometimes reclined
on couches.

Supper could include:

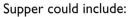

Bread – leavened, unleavened, sweetened or unsweetened.

Fish – salted or dried with a hint of mint or dill.

Chicken – boiled or stewed with rice. Seasoned with a delicious blend of salt, onions, cumin and garlic.

Wild fowl (quail, dove) – boiled or stewed with rice in a rich gravy.

Lamb – stuffed in squash or wrapped in cabbage or grape leaves. Red meat was mostly served only on special occasions. Pork, rabbit and shellfish were unclean and were not allowed to be eaten (*Leviticus 11*).

Soup – thick with peas, beans and lentils.

Porridge – made with freshly-ground corn.

Fruit, nuts and cheese – grapes, figs, olives, mulberries, pomegranates, apricots, plums, oranges, lemons, melons, dates, almonds, walnuts and cheese curds. Fruit and vegetables were bought fresh from the market when needed.

Extras – boiled or roast locusts, fried grasshoppers, roast corn.

Dessert – dried figs boiled in grape molasses, honeycombs, honey doughnuts, locust biscuits, fig and cinnamon cakes.

Drinks – water, red wine, honey wine, goats' milk, grape juice. Drinking water was sold on the street in goatskins.

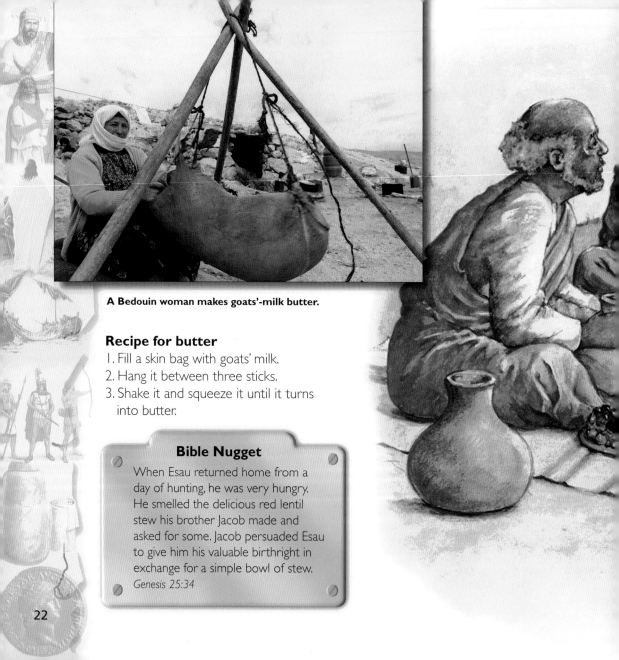

A Bedouin woman makes goats'-milk butter.

Recipe for butter

1. Fill a skin bag with goats' milk.
2. Hang it between three sticks.
3. Shake it and squeeze it until it turns into butter.

Bible Nugget

When Esau returned home from a day of hunting, he was very hungry. He smelled the delicious red lentil stew his brother Jacob made and asked for some. Jacob persuaded Esau to give him his valuable birthright in exchange for a simple bowl of stew.
Genesis 25:34

A family enjoys their evening meal together. What are they eating?

promised themselves to each other. This was similar to engagement today.

■ *The Contract*: The betrothal was made in writing. It was a binding, legal arrangement.

Weddings

Marriages were usually arranged by the parents. It was customary for a son's mother and father to choose his wife. If both families agreed with the arrangement, and if the son's family could pay the "dowry" (bride-price), the wedding took place.

The amount of the dowry depended upon what the bride was worth and how much the family could afford. Gold or silver was typical, but the dowry could also be paid in jewels, animals, goods or service (*1 Samuel 18:22–25; Genesis 34:12*). Fifty shekels was the usual price for a new bride. A widow or divorced woman was worth only half that amount.

Betrothal (*Genesis 19:14*)
■ *The Promise*: One year before a man and woman married, they

A Yemenite bride in her wedding headdress.

24

Brides of Bible times wore decorative clothing like this.

■ *The Gift*: Jewels, usually semi-precious stones set in gold, were given to the bride-to-be and sometimes to her mother too. The dowry could be paid at this time.

Girls were usually betrothed between 13 and 17 years of age; their husbands-to-be were generally young men around 17 or 18 years old.

Wedding wear

■ *Kallah* (bride): Fine linen, embroidered with gold thread. The bride's hair was often braided with jewels. Her headdress was adorned with gemstones, gold ornaments and later with gold and silver coins. Some brides wore a crown of flowers.

25

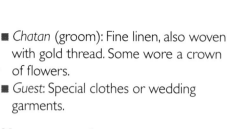

- *Chatan* (groom): Fine linen, also woven with gold thread. Some wore a crown of flowers.
- *Guest*: Special clothes or wedding garments.

Here comes the groom

1. On the wedding day, the bride waited for her groom to arrive. Her attendants lit clay oil-lamps so that the house stayed bright as evening approached.
2. The groom and his friends walked to the bride's home carrying torches.
3. Together, they led a joyful procession through the village, with musicians playing drums and tambourines, torch-bearers, dancers, family and friends.
4. A feast was held at the groom's house, and the new couple was blessed by their parents.

- The bride and groom wore crowns because they were proclaimed "king and queen" of the marriage festivities (*Song of Solomon 3:11*).
- Wedding traditions varied. Sometimes a separate feast was held for the bride and for the groom. Feasts could last between seven and fourteen days, depending on the wealth of the families.
- Most weddings took place when the full harvest was in. Entire villages were often invited. It was considered very rude to turn down an invitation to a wedding.

Which son of Isaac and Rebekah worked fourteen years for his future father-in-law to marry the woman he loved?
Answer: Jacob. He worked seven years for Laban for the right to wed Rachel. On their wedding night, Laban switched his older daughter Leah for Rachel. Jacob agreed to serve another seven years to pay a second dowry for Rachel (*Genesis 29:16–30*).

Bible Nugget

While Jesus was attending a wedding at Cana in Galilee, the bridegroom ran out of wine for his guests. To save the groom embarrassment, Jesus changed the water in six stone jars into a fine wine.

John 2:6–11

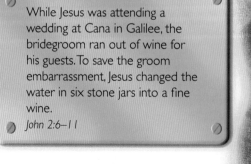

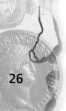

Bride and groom feast under a special canopy at their wedding banquet.

27

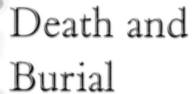

Death and Burial

It was a very sad time when a loved one died. If possible, all work stopped for about a week. Generally mourning lasted for at least a month.

- Bodies were washed, rubbed with oil and sprinkled with perfume, aloes and spices. They were wrapped in long linen strips.
- Burials usually took place within eight hours. Jews thought it was shameful for a body to stay in the land of the living when the soul had already returned to God.
- Bodies were carried through the town on biers or stretchers. Mourners, including family and friends, made a procession through the streets. Flutes were often played.
- Anyone who touched a dead body was "ceremonially unclean" for seven days. They had to be made clean in a special ceremony (Numbers 19:11–13).

- The dead person's house was also "unclean" for seven days. No food was allowed to be prepared there during that time. Friends brought in meals for the family.
- After a period of time, bones were taken from their graves and placed in a stone box called an "ossuary".

Expressions of Mourning

- Mourners wore sackcloth made of black goats' hair, which they tore to express their grief. It was coarse and uncomfortable. Their discomfort wearing it expressed the discomfort of their grief (2 Samuel 1:2).
- Dust and ashes were sprinkled on the head (Joshua 7:6).

An ossuary or "bone box" from New Testament times.

- The head and lower part of the face were sometimes covered with a veil (*Jeremiah 14:3*).
- In earlier times, heads or beards were shaved.
- Family and friends gathered around the body and wailed.
- Professional mourners were hired by the family to help express public grief (*Matthew 9:23*).

Graves and Tombs

- Graves for ordinary people were in open fields outside the city. They were usually situated on any side except the west, since winds blew from that direction (*Luke 7:12*).
- There were private family cemeteries, but the poor were buried in common public graves (*Genesis 47:29–30; Jeremiah 26:23*).
- Hebrew graves were holes in the ground, natural caves or tombs carved from rock. Tombs were often big enough for people to walk inside (*Genesis 35:8*).
- Tombs were sealed by large boulders to keep out wild animals. Boulders were painted white to warn strangers to keep away (*Matthew 23:27*).
- Kings and prophets were buried within the city gates, in more elaborate tombs with several chambers.

The "tomb of Absalom", Jerusalem.

Bible Nugget

When Lazarus died, he was buried in a tomb with a stone laid across the entrance. His friends and family were weeping and wailing. Even though Lazarus had been dead for four days, Jesus commanded him to "come out". Lazarus walked out of the tomb, still covered in his grave clothes!
John 11:1–44.

Jewish Rulers of Old Testament Times

The Israelites had a very long history, dating back to the time of Abraham. As their numbers grew and the years passed, their type of government often changed to meet the changing needs of the people.

Rulers of the Israelites

1. God

When Moses led the Israelites out of Egypt, God was their ruler. Moses received instructions and laws directly from God and passed them on to the people (*Exodus 19:5–8*).

2. Elders

A group of elders was chosen to represent the people during the wilderness journey. Later, they ruled communities and made major decisions (*Ruth 4:1–4*).

Gideon, a "judge of Israel", leads an army against the Midianites.

Moses and Aaron tell Pharaoh to let their people go.

3. Judges

The Israelites settled in Canaan and were ruled by judges for several hundred years. These men and women led during peacetime and were also leaders in war. Famous judges include Deborah, Gideon and Samson (*Judges 2:18*).

   God told Moses to make sure that "cities of refuge" were scattered throughout the Promised Land.

Young David – the future king of Israel – fights the gigantic Goliath in single combat.

If someone committed a crime by accident, they were allowed to hide in one of these cities until they had been given a fair trial (*Joshua 20*).

4. Kings

The Israelites decided they wanted a king, as other countries had. Saul was the first. There were good kings such as David and his son Solomon. There were also bad kings such as Jeroboam (*1 Samuel 8:5*).

Saul, the first king of Israel.

Solomon, the famously wise king of Israel.

5. Conquering countries

The kingdom of Israel was often conquered by foreign armies. When the Syrians controlled Israel, they allowed the Jewish high priest to rule the land. He was, however, always subject to Syria.

Bible Nugget

King Solomon divided the kingdom of Israel into twelve districts and appointed a governor for each one. Each governor was in charge of supplying provisions for the king and his royal household for one month of the year.

1 Kings 4:7

Ruling Palestine in New Testament Times

Official documents would have been written on scrolls like this.

There was endless fighting in Palestine. In 63 BC, the Roman government decided the only way to bring peace to the land was to occupy it.

Roman Rule
King Herod the Great

Under the Romans, Herod ruled most of Palestine. Though he was half-Jewish, the Jews hated him. He rebuilt the temple, but also ordered all infant boys in Bethlehem to be put to death, in an attempt to kill baby Jesus (*Matthew 2:1–18*).

The Colosseum, near Rome's central forum.

Herod's sons

Herod died, and the country was divided into three areas. These were ruled by Herod's three sons: Archelaus (Judea and Samaria), Herod Antipas (Galilee) and Philip (Iturea) (*Matthew 2:19–23*).

When Judea was made a Roman province, a Roman governor ("procurator") was put in charge. Pontius Pilate ruled during the days of Jesus (*Matthew 27:1, 2*).

Some good things about Roman rule

- Roman rule brought peace to a region plagued by civil war. This order lasted about five centuries.
- Romans knew the wisest way to govern Palestine was to give the Jews some space. They tried to be tolerant of their customs and religious practices.
- The Roman army built paved roads which made travel easier. Their presence also did

Herod the Great.

away with many of the bandits who threatened travel. This allowed trade to flourish and the Christian gospel to be spread through much of the ancient world.

Some bad things about Roman rule

- As the emperor became more powerful, Romans began to worship him as a god. They tried to make the Jews say "Caesar is Lord".
- When Christians refused to worship Caesar, they were persecuted. Many were thrown to the lions.

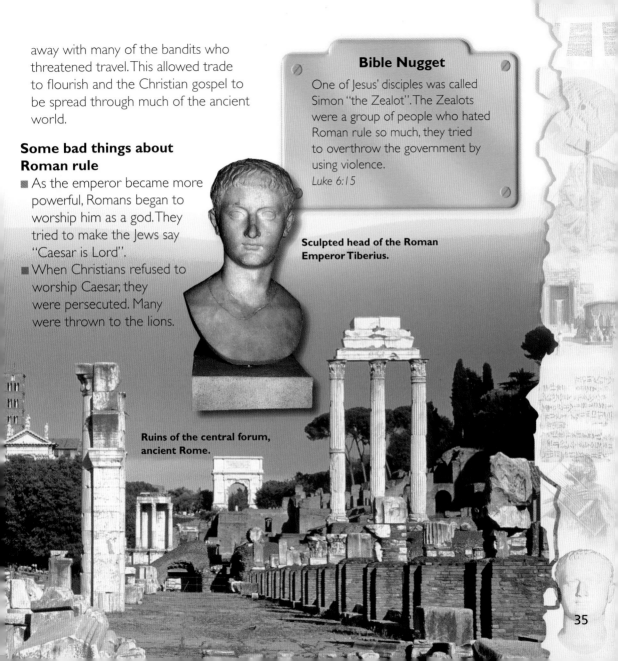

Sculpted head of the Roman Emperor Tiberius.

Ruins of the central forum, ancient Rome.

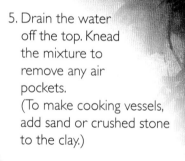

The Potter

Pottery-making is one of the oldest and most important crafts. Nearly every village had a potter. Potters made storage jars, bowls, plates, cups, basins, cooking pots, decanters, flasks, jugs, lamps, ovens and seals for letters.

How to make pottery
Making the clay

1. Dig up some clay dust from a field or wet clay from a stream bank (*Matthew 27:7*).
2. Let it weather in the sun for a day or two.
3. Pound out the lumps with a mallet. Pick out the twigs and pebbles.
4. Add water and mix it with your feet until it's smooth (*Isaiah 41:25*).

5. Drain the water off the top. Knead the mixture to remove any air pockets.
(To make cooking vessels, add sand or crushed stone to the clay.)

How to shape the clay

1. Shape the clay by hand. Try making long sausage-like rolls and coiling them up. Or press sheets of clay into wooden forms.

The Dead Sea Scrolls were discovered in clay pots like this.

A potter of Bible times. How is he turning his wheel?

2. Try out the potter's wheel (*Lamentations 4:2*).
3. Let the pieces dry. Trim off any extra material.

How to decorate the clay

1. Use a knife to make decorative marks in your piece.
2. Brush the container with "slip" – creamy clay – to smooth the surface.
3. Rub your piece with a stone to make it shiny.
4. Try painting on decorations, pressing the clay with a woven rope to make an interesting pattern or adding other pieces of clay.

Pots and jars from Bible times.

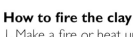

How to fire the clay

1. Make a fire or heat up the kiln. Bake your pieces at between 700° and 1050° centigrade for up to three days.
2. Now you're ready to sell your pottery in the marketplace!

■ The earliest clay pots were baked in the sun. They were brittle and broke easily. Later it was discovered that "firing" pots made them harder and longer-lasting.

■ The first potter's wheels were made of wood – then stone.

■ Painted pottery from Jerusalem was fragile and thin. Red bowls from Jerusalem were luxury goods like fine china today. People felt fortunate if they could afford to buy a complete set.

A Roman oil-lamp made of clay. What does the decoration show?

Two ancient wine jars, or amphoras. Such jars would have been loaded on Roman merchant ships to transport wine and olive oil. The long pointed shaft would be slotted into a vertical hole in the deck to prevent the jar shifting at sea.

Bible Nugget

God told Jeremiah to go to the potter's house. There the prophet saw a potter shaping and reshaping a pot at his wheel. God said he wished Israel was like a piece of clay that he could shape in his hands, changing it until it was just right.

Jeremiah 18:1–6

The Tanner (Leatherworker)

Tanners made leather from animal hides. While this was an important trade, tanners were sometimes avoided because their contact with dead animals made them ceremonially "unclean", regarded as unfit to worship God.

How to prepare a hide

1. Soak animal skins (usually sheep, goat, badger, ram, jackal or hyena) for several days in a bath of water and old lime.
2. Rinse the skins until the water runs clean.
3. Stretch the skins on a round frame and let them dry.
4. Scrape the skins with a sharp knife, removing as many hairs as possible. Rub with pumice, then with animal manure.

A leatherworker making sandals.

39

5. Hammer the skins until soft and flat.

Tanners had to locate their shops on the outskirts of town, because they were "unclean", and also so the wind wouldn't carry nasty smells into town.

When animals were sacrificed in the temple, their skins were divided up among the priests. They often sold them to the tanners.

Some objects made of leather:
- hyena- or jackal-hide ankle boots
- sandal laces, straps and belts
- writing materials, water- and wine-bottles, slings, helmets and shields.

Goatskin was used to make leather.

A pair of leather sandals.

Bible Nugget

God sent a vision to the Roman centurion Cornelius. He was to call for Peter, who was staying at the home of Simon the tanner. Even though Simon was seen as "unclean", Peter knew that he was clean in God's eyes and worth spending time with.

Acts 9:43

The Carpenter

Carpentry was an important trade. At least one carpenter could be found in each large village and town. Most carpenters – like Joseph of Nazareth – earned a living making things such as roofs, window shutters and yokes. They also made furniture, including tables, chairs and storage boxes.

Nazareth was known as a town of carpenters. A carpenter often displayed

Joseph, the carpenter of Nazareth.

his trade by wearing a wood-chip tucked behind his ear.

Transporting logs on the river.

Ancient Egyptian toolbox

An ancient Egyptian used all these tools:
axe – to chop wood
adze – to shape the wood
saw – to cut wood to exact size
square – to make right-angles

awl – to make small holes in wood
plumb line – to make sure a wall was
  upright
hammer
glue-pot.

Joseph of Nazareth's toolbox

Centuries later, in the time of Joseph,
carpenters used these tools too:
bow-drill and bits – to drill holes in wood
stone-headed hammer – to drive in nails
wooden mallet – to hammer wooden
  pieces together
iron chisels/files – to shape and carve
  wood
ruler and compass – to measure
wood plane – to smooth or shape
spokeshave – to slice off thin shavings
nails.

Wood often used by carpenters

■ The woods used most often in
  Palestine were soft Jerusalem sycamore,
  hard olive wood and oak.
■ Cedar imported from Lebanon was
  very expensive. It was used for the
  palaces and temples of David, Solomon
  and Herod.
■ Algum wood from India was also used
  in Solomon's Temple. It was black
  outside, ruby red on the inside and
  smelled sweet.

By Appointment to the King

King Hiram of Tyre sent King David skilled
Phoenician carpenters to help build his
royal palace (*2 Samuel 5:11*).
Solomon used the finest carpenters to
build the Temple (*Ezra 3:7*).

**Carpenter's tools from Bible
times. Do you know what
each tool was used for?**

A carpenter of Bible times.
What is he making?

43

Nazareth, where Joseph worked as a carpenter.

Josiah employed carpenters to help repair the damaged Temple (*2 Kings 22:5–6*). *Herod the Great* used carpenters to shape doors and window frames for use in his Temple in Jerusalem.

Bible Nugget

When Jesus was preaching in his hometown of Nazareth, the people were amazed by his wisdom and the miracles he performed. They had a hard time believing that Jesus, the son of a carpenter, could really be the son of God.
Mark 6:3

Carpenters at work with a saw and a drill.

Spinning and Weaving

Spinners turned materials such as wool, flax and cotton into thread or yarn. Weavers then used the thread or yarn to weave cloth and rugs.

How to spin

1. Wind a bundle of wool, flax or cotton around a stick called a "distaff". Hold it in your left hand or put it in your belt.
2. Hold a spindle (a long, tapering rod) in the right hand. Wind the thread from the distaff onto the spindle, twisting as you go.

- The first spindles were made of stone.
- Thread or yarn was dyed different hues, either at home or by the local dyer.

- In Jesus' day, most looms produced cloth only about one metre (three feet) wide. Two pieces of cloth had to be sewn together to make cloth wide enough to fit the average person.
- Weavers also wove reeds and rushes into baskets.

Textiles of ancient times
Cotton

- Cotton was imported from Persia into the Holy Land.
- Cotton was used to make the lining for woollen tunics, long underwear, caps and headscarves.
- The Egyptians wove cotton into special cloth to wrap up their mummies.

Simple weaving in the open air.

Wool

- Wool was one of the first materials used to make cloth.
- Wool was used for tunics, cloaks, girdles (sashes), caps, headscarves and cords.
- Wool from the city of Damascus was famous for its whiteness and fetched good prices at market (*Ezekiel 27:18*).

Linen

- Linen was made from the flax plant, grown in Egypt and Israel. It was common to see flax drying on sunny rooftops (*Joshua 2:6*).
- Linen was used to make priests' clothing, tunics, girdles (sashes), turbans, napkins and lamp wicks. The fabric was strong and kept the wearer cool in the hot desert sun.
- Egyptian linen was fine and white. Pharaoh dressed Joseph in linen after he called for him from prison (*Genesis 41:42*).
- Wearing linen was a sign of wealth (*Luke 16:19*).

How to weave

1. Fasten a spool of thread to the shuttle of the loom.
2. Pass it from side to side, moving it over and under the vertical threads. In this way tightly-woven cloth is formed.

Bible Nugget

Wives who spun were thought to be good. Weavers were regarded as master craftsmen and designers.
Proverbs 31:19; Exodus 35:35

A weaver of Bible times. Notice her spare reels of wool.

Clothing

Clothing was made of cotton, wool or silk, depending on the wealth of the wearer.

Women's clothing
- Undergarment – long and tied with a sash.
- Gown – long and fringed, sometimes with pointy sleeves.
- Jacket – small, tight-fitting, sometimes embroidered.
- Headdress – a plain shawl or scarf.

Men's clothing
- Undergarment – sometimes short like a vest, or undershirt, sometimes long.
- Tunic coat – sometimes worn to the ankle.
- Girdle – a cloth or leather sash worn around the tunic. The folds of a cloth girdle acted like a pocket to carry change, nuts and other small things.

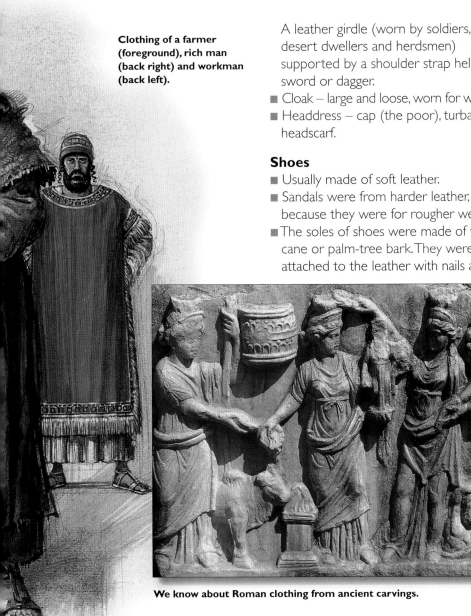

Clothing of a farmer (foreground), rich man (back right) and workman (back left).

A leather girdle (worn by soldiers, desert dwellers and herdsmen) supported by a shoulder strap held a sword or dagger.

- Cloak – large and loose, worn for warmth.
- Headdress – cap (the poor), turban or headscarf.

Shoes

- Usually made of soft leather.
- Sandals were from harder leather, because they were for rougher wear.
- The soles of shoes were made of wood, cane or palm-tree bark. They were attached to the leather with nails and

We know about Roman clothing from ancient carvings.

49

tied around the feet with thongs (*Genesis 14:23*).

■ Most men had at least two pairs of shoes.

Which piece of clothing was the most important for a man?
His cloak, sometimes called a mantle or robe. The cloak was used as a coat, a blanket and even as a saddle-cloth. God said if you took someone's cloak as a pledge, to return it by sunset. It was the only covering for the man's body (*Exodus 22:26–27*).

Adornment

Adornments included earrings, nose rings and nose jewels, signet rings, toe rings, anklets, bracelets and necklaces (*Isaiah 3:18; Genesis 24:22*).

■ Men wore earrings and rings.

■ Expensive jewels were crafted from gold, silver, ivory and precious stones, such as red garnets and blue sapphires. Cheaper jewels were made from bronze and glass.

■ Jewels were taken as part of war booty, and also given as betrothal gifts (*Genesis 24:30*).

■ High priests wore a breast-piece studded with precious stones. High officials wore gold chains (*Exodus 39; Genesis 41:42*).

Clothing of Bible times. Notice the rich man's fancy sandals.

Carving depicting a Roman woman's cosmetics tray.

A rich couple of Bible times. Notice the woman's adornments.

Make-up

Women painted their eyes, cheeks and mouths. They also used a yellowish-orange paste on their fingernails and the palms of their hands (*2 Kings 9:30*).

Hair Care

Women did not wear long hair loose in public, but braided it with flowers, ribbons and jewels. They used gold and ivory combs, gold hairpins and ribbons, gold hairnets, headbands and tiaras, if they were rich enough.

Men, in Old Testament times, wore hair long with a beard if Hebrew or Arab, and shaved their beard if Egyptian (*Genesis 41:14*). In New Testament times Jewish men wore hair short and never clipped the edges of their beard (*Leviticus 19:27*).

Costume of a farmer's wife (foreground) and rich woman.

Bible Nugget

Peter warns us that beauty does not come from outward adornments such as braided hair, gold jewels and fine clothes. Rather, true beauty comes from a gentle, quiet spirit which is highly valued in God's eyes.
1 Peter 3:3

Farming

The Canaanites who lived in Palestine before the Israelites arrived were good farmers and the Israelites learned from them.

It was not possible to cultivate the more mountainous or the driest parts of the land. The commonest cereal crops were wheat and barley, while the most popular fruits were olives, vines and figs.

A farmer winnows his grain.

A small olive press.

53

A farmer harvests his grain with a sickle.

54

The land in Palestine was so rich that there was no need to fertilize it. Every seventh year, farms, olive orchards and vineyards were supposed to lie in fallow, or rest.

When Egypt fell under Roman rule in 30 BC, Egyptian farmers provided most of the grain needed to feed people in the entire Roman empire!

Some common farming terms

Sickle: the tool used to cut grain. First made of flint, later of metal.

Threshing: a process to separate the grain from the stalks. The stalks are beaten with a rod or trampled under the feet of oxen.

Threshing floor: place where grain is threshed, usually clay soil packed hard and smooth.

Winnowing: a process to separate the valuable seeds of grain from the light, useless "chaff". Piles of threshed grain are scooped up with a winnowing-fork and tossed into the air. The grain falls close, the lighter straw further away. The lightest chaff blows away in the breeze.

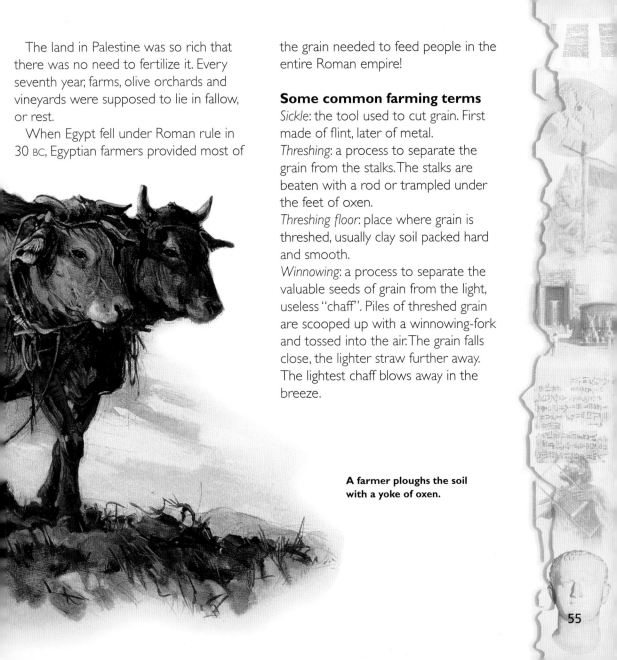

A farmer ploughs the soil with a yoke of oxen.

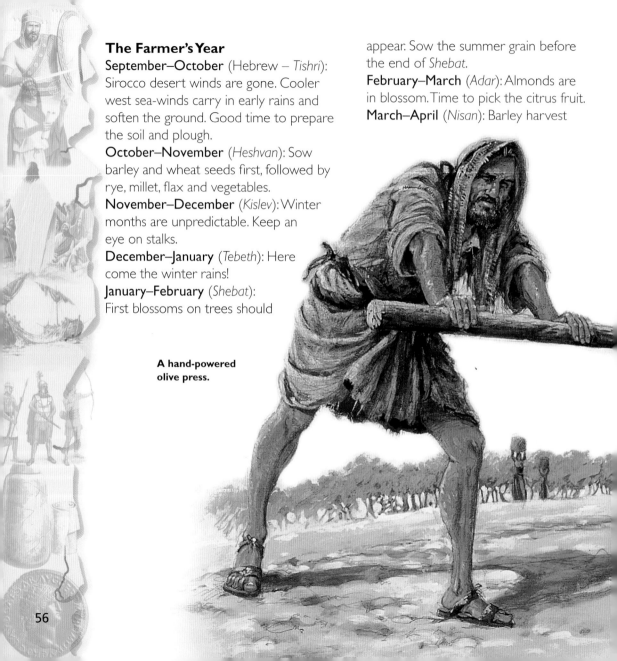

The Farmer's Year

September–October (Hebrew – *Tishri*): Sirocco desert winds are gone. Cooler west sea-winds carry in early rains and soften the ground. Good time to prepare the soil and plough.

October–November (*Heshvan*): Sow barley and wheat seeds first, followed by rye, millet, flax and vegetables.

November–December (*Kislev*): Winter months are unpredictable. Keep an eye on stalks.

December–January (*Tebeth*): Here come the winter rains!

January–February (*Shebat*): First blossoms on trees should appear. Sow the summer grain before the end of *Shebat*.

February–March (*Adar*): Almonds are in blossom. Time to pick the citrus fruit.

March–April (*Nisan*): Barley harvest

A hand-powered olive press.

A farmer loosens the soil with a donkey-drawn plough.

57

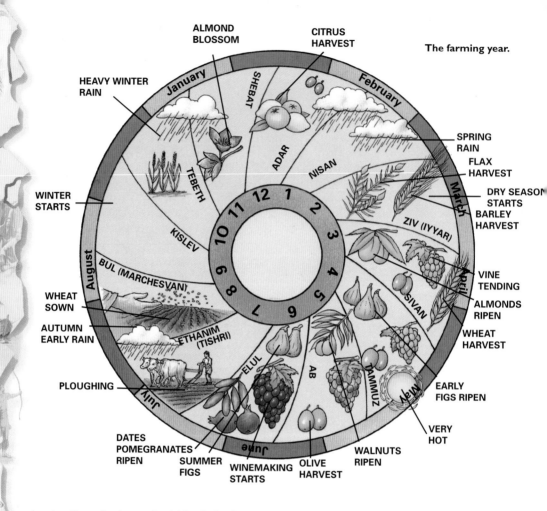

The farming year.

ALMOND BLOSSOM

CITRUS HARVEST

HEAVY WINTER RAIN

SPRING RAIN

FLAX HARVEST

DRY SEASON STARTS BARLEY HARVEST

WINTER STARTS

VINE TENDING

ALMONDS RIPEN

WHEAT SOWN

WHEAT HARVEST

AUTUMN EARLY RAIN

EARLY FIGS RIPEN

PLOUGHING

VERY HOT

DATES POMEGRANATES RIPEN

SUMMER FIGS

WINEMAKING STARTS

OLIVE HARVEST

WALNUTS RIPEN

SHEBAT
ADAR
NISAN
ZIV (IYYAR)
SIVAN
TEBETH
KISLEV
BUL (MARCHESVAN)
ETHANIM (TISHRI)
ELUL
AB
TAMMUZ

January · February · March · April · May · June · July · August

12 11 10 9 8 7 6 5 4 3 2 1

begins. Pray for late rains. Watch for hot east winds with the coming of the dry season, as well as occasional hail storms. **April–May** (*Iyyar*): Barley harvest. Guard against pests such as palmerworm,

cankerworm, caterpillar and locust which will kill your crops.
May–June (*Sivan*): Wheat harvest. Beware of crows, sparrows and fungus. Vintage (grape) season begins.

June–July (*Tammuz*): Grapes, figs and olives ripen under the hot summer sun. Tend to vines.

Bible Nugget

Wise King Solomon tells us, "There is a time for everything, and a season for every activity under heaven: a time to be born and a time to die, a time to plant, and a time to uproot."
Ecclesiastes 3:1–2

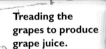

Treading the grapes to produce grape juice.

Harvesting the grapes.

59

The Shepherd

The shepherd tended his or other people's sheep and goats. Often, shepherds were hired by rich owners.

- The shepherd led his animals from oasis to oasis in search of food and water.
- Whenever possible, he kept the herds in a protective fold at night.
- He watched for wild beasts and wandering strays, sometimes from a watchtower.

A shepherd in hills near Bethlehem.

A shepherd leads his flock back to the fold.

The shepherd's crook could be used to rescue sheep.

The sheep market at Beersheba, southern Israel.

Since shepherds were always on the move, they carried only:

- a portable shelter, usually a tent
- a long cloak that doubled as a blanket
- a small bag for provisions
- a sharp crook, goad or pole for prodding the animals.

Milking a goat. Goats' milk was used to make butter, cheese and yogurt.

A shepherd's watchtower near Bethlehem.

63

Fishermen

Fishermen spent most of their time on the Sea of Galilee, a large, freshwater lake. Since fish was a large part of the diet, the fisherman was very important. Fish were salted, pickled, dried and sold or traded with other countries.

Night fishing was common. Fishermen dragged a torch above the water to attract the fish to the surface. They began at dusk and returned at sunrise with their catch.

Even today fishing remains good on the Sea of Galilee. Up to thirty-seven kinds of fish can be found in these waters. *Tilapia galilea* and sardines abound, and herring and salmon can be caught with a dragnet. The barbel, blenny and eel-like silurus can be found too.

The Sea of Galilee

The Sea of Galilee is 21 km (13 miles) long, 13 km (8 miles) wide and 45 metres (150 feet) deep in parts and lies

Two fishing boats work together to pull in a net filled with fish.

Fishing on Galilee.

65

Fishing on Galilee in the nineteenth century.

209 metres (685 feet) below sea level. Fresh water flows in from the River Jordan. Weather around the lake is unpredictable. Calm conditions are typical on most mornings, but late afternoons

A fisherman using a casting net.

can bring sudden, violent storms with 6 metre (20 foot) waves.

Fishing boats on the Sea of Galilee were sturdy. They had oars, probably a central sail and could hold up to a dozen men.

Peter's fishing surprise

In the Sea of Galilee Jesus' disciple Peter caught a *Tilapia galilea* (often called "St. Peter's fish") with a silver coin in its mouth (*Matthew 17:27*)!

Types of fishing net

■ *Dragnet*: very heavy, needing several men to work. The net was let down over the side of the boat, and floats marked its location in the water. Then it was pulled to the shore or into the boat, hopefully filled with fish.

Mosaic of a fishing boat on Galilee.

Fishermen prepare their nets on Galilee.

Most nets were edged with weights so that they would sink into the water.

Hooks and harpoons were also used sometimes (*Matthew 17:27*).

As well as cleaning and sorting the fish, fishermen spent time mending torn nets (*Matthew 4:21*).

- *Hand net or casting net*: a small, circular net thrown from the shore or shallow water.
- *Bag net*: used to trap fish in deep water.

Bible Nugget

Simon Peter, James and John returned from a night of fishing with empty nets. When Jesus told them to cast their nets again into the deep water of the Sea of Galilee, they were dubious but obeyed. When they returned, their nets were breaking from the weight of all the fish that they had caught!

Luke 5:1–7

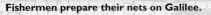

This Galilee fishing boat dates from around the time of Jesus.

The Merchant

Merchants journeyed far and wide to find goods that people needed or wanted. In ancient times, they traded their goods door to door. Later, they set up shop in the marketplaces of villages and towns.

Journeying merchants stopped at inns called "caravansaries" along major trade routes. A caravansary offered shelter, water and rest during a long journey. Merchants would swap stories and pass on news when staying overnight.

Sometimes merchants set up temporary shop at the city gate, where people gathered. Shops were often crowded side by side. Shops selling similar goods were grouped together.

Merchants often used beam-balances to weigh their goods, and charged accordingly.

Remains of an ancient caravansary.

A busy marketplace in Bible times. What goods are being sold?

A city gate, where merchants often traded their goods.

Market inspectors checked the merchants' scales to be sure they weighed correctly. They also made sure prices were fair. "Crooked" merchants were not uncommon.

Some customers only shopped with merchants who used the "king's weights" – approved by the authorities.

Merchants had to borrow from money-lenders to pay for the cost of their goods and for space on board a ship.

Some food and drink sold at market:
- artichokes and pickled fish from Spain
- truffles from Jerusalem
- plums and figs from Palestine and Africa
- dates from Jericho's date palms
- goats' cheese and honey from Sicily
- barley and wheat from Egypt

Vegetables for sale in Bethlehem market.

- oil from Palestine and Italy
- wine from Palestine, Gaul and Greece
- spicy pepper from India.

Other market goods:

- papyrus from Egypt
- silks and cottons from China and India
- rugs from Asia Minor
- frankincense and myrrh from Arabia
- cloth from Britain
- glass goblets and bowls from Syria.

Bible Nugget

The prophet Micah compared Israel to a merchant who uses dishonest scales and false weights. Both will be punished.

Micah 6:11

Grains, pulses and nuts for sale in Beersheba market.

Travel

Most people went on foot or on a donkey. The poor could not afford a carriage or a camel (*1 Samuel 25:18*). Travel was a risky business, especially for those on foot. Thieves hid along the roads and waited for an opportunity to ambush people journeying past (*Judges 9:25*).

Camels are well adapted to travel across hot, dry deserts.

Travel options
Camel
- Could cover 40 to 50 km (25 to 30 miles) per day.
- Could carry 180 kilos (400 lbs) of goods.
- Could survive more than two weeks without water and walk through windstorms and on hot sand.

The chariot of an Assyrian king.

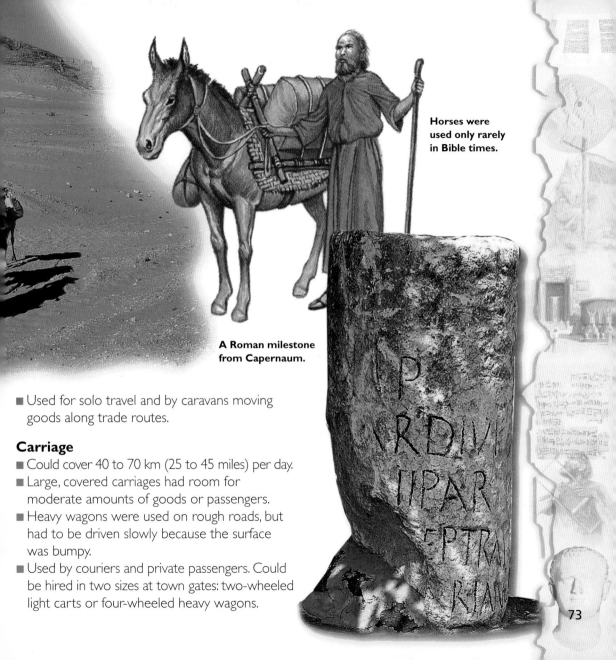

**Horses were
used only rarely
in Bible times.**

**A Roman milestone
from Capernaum.**

■ Used for solo travel and by caravans moving
goods along trade routes.

Carriage
■ Could cover 40 to 70 km (25 to 45 miles) per day.
■ Large, covered carriages had room for
moderate amounts of goods or passengers.
■ Heavy wagons were used on rough roads, but
had to be driven slowly because the surface
was bumpy.
■ Used by couriers and private passengers. Could
be hired in two sizes at town gates: two-wheeled
light carts or four-wheeled heavy wagons.

73

A Roman two-horse passenger carriage.

A Roman road in biblical times. From left to right: a donkey carrying a farmer and his produce; a horse-drawn passenger carriage; a horse-drawn chariot; a Roman cavalry officer and a large horse-drawn carriage.

Mule or donkey

- Could cover 30 or more km (20 miles) per day.
- Could carry or pull heavy loads.
- Sure-footed on mountainous routes and could endure long journeys.
- Used for personal travel and to carry goods on trade routes.

On foot

- Could cover 24 to 30 km (15 to 20 miles) per day.
- Could carry small load on back, according to the age and health of the walker.
- Could travel on rough or smooth terrain.

Horse

- Could cover 40 to 50 km (25 to 30 miles) per day.
- Could carry moderate load.
- Stirrups were unknown and saddles were blankets.
- Horses were rarely used for travel: they were too expensive and too uncomfortable.

Litter

- Could cover only a few kilometres per day.
- No use for carrying goods.
- Designed to be luxurious, not durable.

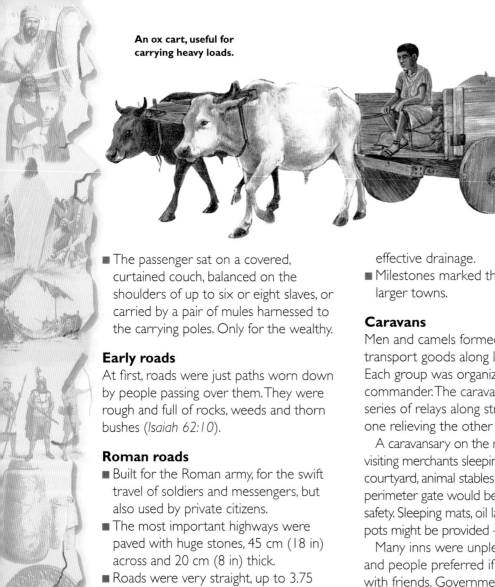

An ox cart, useful for carrying heavy loads.

■ The passenger sat on a covered, curtained couch, balanced on the shoulders of up to six or eight slaves, or carried by a pair of mules harnessed to the carrying poles. Only for the wealthy.

Early roads
At first, roads were just paths worn down by people passing over them. They were rough and full of rocks, weeds and thorn bushes (*Isaiah 62:10*).

Roman roads
■ Built for the Roman army, for the swift travel of soldiers and messengers, but also used by private citizens.
■ The most important highways were paved with huge stones, 45 cm (18 in) across and 20 cm (8 in) thick.
■ Roads were very straight, up to 3.75 metres (12 feet) wide, and sloping for effective drainage.
■ Milestones marked the distance to larger towns.

Caravans
Men and camels formed "caravans" to transport goods along land trade routes. Each group was organized by a caravan commander. The caravans moved in a series of relays along stretches of desert, one relieving the other at a certain point.

A caravansary on the route offered visiting merchants sleeping rooms, a courtyard, animal stables and a well. The perimeter gate would be locked at night for safety. Sleeping mats, oil lamps and chamber pots might be provided – but not food.

Many inns were unpleasant and unsafe and people preferred if possible to stay with friends. Government officers and other important people stayed at the homes of local officials.

Caravan imports

Some goods from distant countries had first to be shipped to a port. At the port, the goods were loaded onto a caravan that carried them along inland trade routes.

Goods included:

- frankincense and myrrh from Arabia
- fine rugs and embroideries from Asia Minor (modern Turkey)
- spices, drugs, ivory, cotton and silks from India, China and Africa
- bitumen (petroleum tar) from Mesopotamia (modern Iraq).

The decorated chariot of an important official.

How did people on the move keep in touch with their family back home? The wealthy had personal couriers, but most people found someone going in the right direction who was willing to carry their mail. A letter would be written on a sheet of paper and rolled up or folded. The letter was tied, then sealed with a piece of wax impressed with a person's private seal.

A litter could cover a mile or two at most.

Bible Nugget

Inns were not necessary in very ancient times. People lived by the "rule of hospitality". People on their travels were invited into other family homes, where they were fed, refreshed and given somewhere to sleep.
Exodus 2:20

Sea Travel

The Israelites were rather frightened of the sea. The Philistines, Phoenicians, Greeks and Romans designed and built most of the ships that sailed the Mediterranean and beyond.

Types of sailing ship

- *Great merchant ship*: large vessel with two over-sized oars for rudders, a tiller, square mainsail and sometimes additional sails.
- *Alexandria to Rome freighter*: each could carry 1,200 tonnes (1,300 tons) of grain from Egypt to Rome (*Acts 27:6*).
- *Greek and Roman freighter*: carried 63 to 363 tonnes (70 to 400 tons) of goods.

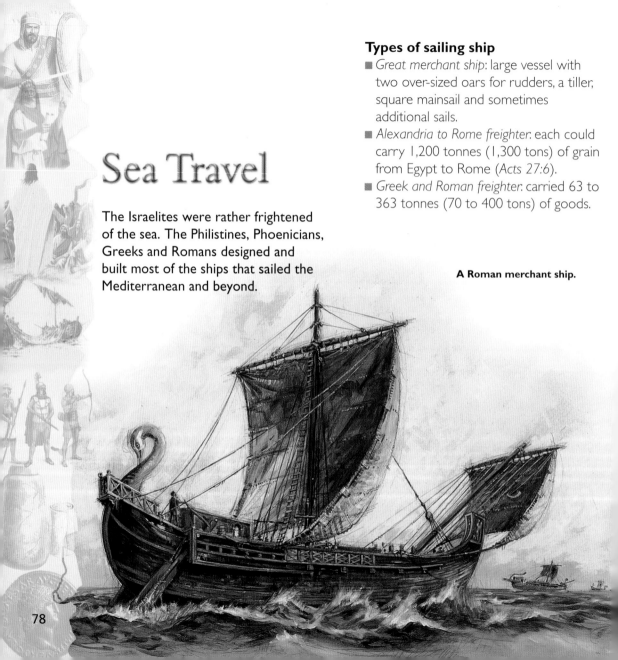

A Roman merchant ship.

Traded up and down the Mediterranean coast, south to Egypt, north to Asia Minor.

- *Ships of Tarshish*: Solomon's fleet of Phoenician ships, sailed by expert Phoenician sailors. Traded to Spain, Ophir and southern India (*1 Kings 9–10*).
- *Merchant galley*: swift, slender vessel, powered and steered by a bank of oars pulled by crews. Usually had a square sail.
- *Phoenician trireme*: invented by the Phoenicians, it had three banks of oars. Sailed to Cornwall, Britain, for tin and to the Canary Islands.
- *Small galley*: used to carry cargo and

Mosaic of a Mediterranean merchant vessel.

Paul meets the captain who is to take him to Rome.

people for short hauls along the coasts or between the islands. Some weren't much bigger than rowboats.

The travel experience

- Passenger vessels didn't exist. People walked up and down the quayside looking for a cargo ship going in their direction that was willing to take them aboard. They had to bring enough food to last the entire trip (*Acts 27:6*).
- In ancient times, captains consulted their passengers before they made big decisions about their voyage. A majority vote ruled (*Acts 27:9–12*).
- Grain was easily carried in sacks or bins.

79

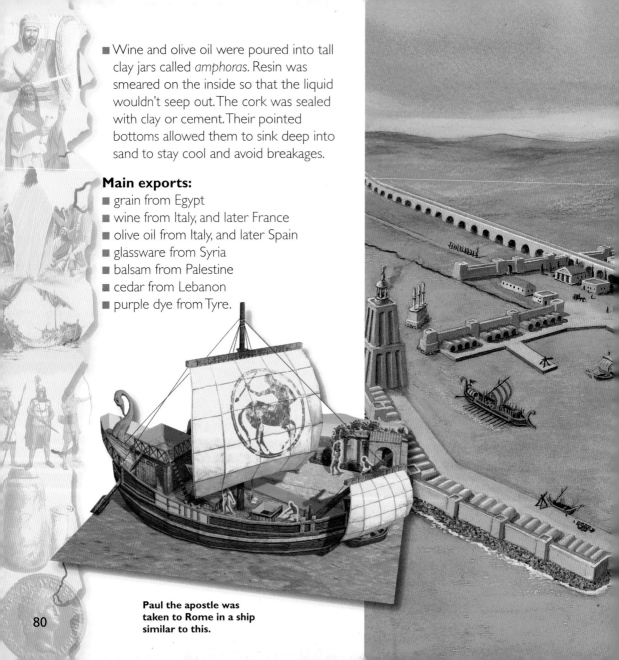

■ Wine and olive oil were poured into tall clay jars called *amphoras*. Resin was smeared on the inside so that the liquid wouldn't seep out. The cork was sealed with clay or cement. Their pointed bottoms allowed them to sink deep into sand to stay cool and avoid breakages.

Main exports:
■ grain from Egypt
■ wine from Italy, and later France
■ olive oil from Italy, and later Spain
■ glassware from Syria
■ balsam from Palestine
■ cedar from Lebanon
■ purple dye from Tyre.

Paul the apostle was taken to Rome in a ship similar to this.

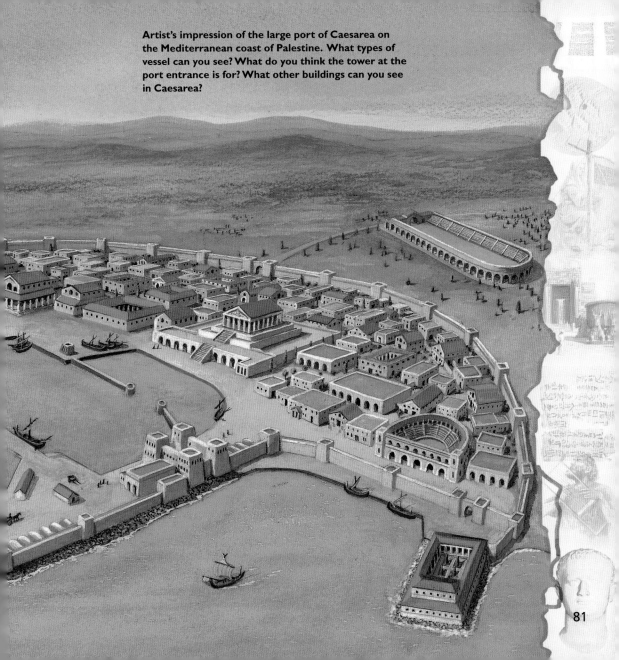

Artist's impression of the large port of Caesarea on the Mediterranean coast of Palestine. What types of vessel can you see? What do you think the tower at the port entrance is for? What other buildings can you see in Caesarea?

Sailors' superstitions

Sailors were very superstitious. Voyages were sometimes delayed or abandoned because of dreams or omens.

Dreams

- Turbulent waters or anchors meant a voyage must be delayed.
- Goats meant big waves and a storm.
- Black goats meant big waves.
- Bulls goring someone meant shipwreck.
- Owls meant storm or pirate attack.

Bad omens

- Someone who sneezes while walking up the gangplank.
- A glimpse of wreckage on shore.
- A crow or magpie croaking in the rigging before the ship left.
- Clipping one's nails during good weather.
- Dancing on board.
- Death aboard ship – the worst omen.

An Egyptian river boat.

Ancient depiction of a Phoenician sea-going galley.

Good omens
- Dreams of walking on water.
- Birds sitting in the rigging during a voyage.

What was the biggest threat to ancient ships apart from shipwreck?
The marine borer, a worm-like creature that tunnels into wood. Sailors nailed thin sheets of lead to the outside of the hull to keep out this pest.

Bible Nugget
During Paul's voyage to Rome aboard a grain ship, he faced turbulent waters and hurricane-strength winds. The ship was tossed about for fourteen days before it was finally wrecked off the coast of Malta. But God spared the lives of all 276 passengers.
Acts 27–28

The Soldier

Over the years, the Israelite army faced many powerful enemies in war. They won great victories when they obeyed God and were defeated when they turned their backs on God.

Marching into Battle

Footmen (infantry): nearly all Israel's early wars were fought by foot soldiers. They carried their weapons and were led into battle by a judge, general or king (*1 Samuel 4:10*).

Horsemen (cavalry): the Israelites were not allowed to keep large numbers of horses (*Deuteronomy 17:16*). Until the time of King David, their armies did not use horsemen (*1 Kings 10:26*).

Charioteers: Egyptian and later Israelite chariots carried two or three soldiers – a driver, an archer or spearman and sometimes a shield-bearer. Assyrian chariots were larger and often held three or four soldiers (*1 Kings 9:22*).

An army was generally divided into two parts:

Division 1
First battle line: spearmen
Second battle line: bowmen or archers
Third battle line: slingers

Division 2
These soldiers brought up the rear. They were used as reserves, and helped the leader to escape if the army was defeated.

■ In ancient times, every Israelite over the age of twenty was a soldier (*Numbers 1:3*).

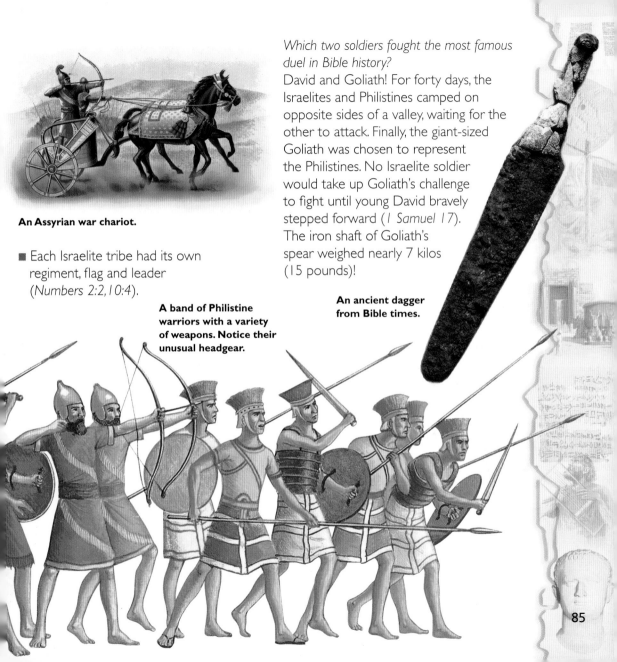

An Assyrian war chariot.

Which two soldiers fought the most famous duel in Bible history?

David and Goliath! For forty days, the Israelites and Philistines camped on opposite sides of a valley, waiting for the other to attack. Finally, the giant-sized Goliath was chosen to represent the Philistines. No Israelite soldier would take up Goliath's challenge to fight until young David bravely stepped forward (*1 Samuel 17*). The iron shaft of Goliath's spear weighed nearly 7 kilos (15 pounds)!

■ Each Israelite tribe had its own regiment, flag and leader (*Numbers 2:2, 10:4*).

A band of Philistine warriors with a variety of weapons. Notice their unusual headgear.

An ancient dagger from Bible times.

Weapons

Bows were made of wood or reed, some almost two metres (five feet) long! Arrows had metal tips. Up to thirty arrows were carried in a quiver. Arrows were sometimes set alight before they were fired.

Clubs were heavy and spiked. They were used to break the enemy's protective clothing. Later, clubs were more like police batons.

Battleaxes were used in hand-to-hand combat.

Swords had long, broad blades used to cut or to thrust. They

Assyrian relief showing a town under siege.

were usually carried in a sheath on a soldier's left side. The Egyptian "*khepesh*" was a crescent-shaped sword.

Left to right: An Israelite archer, Egyptian foot-soldier, Philistine swordsman and Assyrian infantryman.

Dirks were double-edged shorter swords. They were used to slash in hand-to-hand combat. Dirks were carried by Roman soldiers.

Daggers were mostly used for stabbing in hand-to-hand combat.

Spears, javelins, lances and darts were long wooden poles with stone or metal heads. They could be thrown or thrust. Javelins used by Roman legionaries were about two metres (7 feet) long. The iron tip bent on impact and couldn't be reused by enemies.

Slings, made of leather, were wider in the middle to hold a stone. A soldier held both ends in one hand and swung the sling around his head to gain thrust. When he released one end, the stone flew at its target.

Protection

Great shields were big enough to protect the whole body. Made of woven branches or leather, they were treated with oil to preserve them and to allow enemy missiles to slide off them easily (*Isaiah 21:5*).

Bucklers were small, round shields. They were carried by slingers and archers.

Helmets were made of leather, and later bronze. Kings' helmets were sometimes made of gold! Quilted caps kept helmets in place. Roman helmets had flaps to

A Babylonian soldier and Greek warrior (right).

protect the head better.

Coats of mail were made of leather covered with a layer of metal scales. Bronze breastplates, worn under the mail, protected the heart. Roman soldiers wore thick, woollen tunics under their breastplate.

Greaves were metal leg-guards.

An arms-bearer was the personal officer of an army commander. He carried his shield and extra weapons. He was chosen for his bravery and loyalty. Saul, Jonathan, Joab and Goliath all had an arms-bearer (*1 Samuel 31:4*).

A soldier's provisions:

- wheat and barley flour
- roasted grain
- beans and lentils
- honey and curds
- cheese.

The Roman Army

Roman soldiers were well disciplined, organized, paid more and treated better than any other soldiers at this time.

Legionaries: The ordinary fighting men – heavy infantry, cavalry, archers and light infantry. Special soldiers operated *ballistas* that shot huge arrows, and catapults that fired stones. A centurion was commander of a company of about 100 legionaries.

Auxiliaries: Non-Romans recruited into the army from conquered or friendly countries.

The Imperial Guard: Elite soldiers that formed the main force in the city of Rome itself. A few of these soldiers were chosen to guard the emperor:

    a. *The Praetorian Guard* – mostly foot soldiers, heavy infantry, archers and lancers;

    b. *The Imperial Horse Guard* – all horsemen.

The Fleet: Sailors and marines served on board the fleet of the Roman navy.

A Roman centurion (foreground) and legionary. Notice their weaponry.

Their main job was to fight pirates and support the army. These soldiers were in the least prestigious part of the service.

Roman stone carving of a gladiator with his large shield and stumpy dagger.

reward for auxiliary soldiers after at least 25 years' service.

- Roman soldiers relied on the emperor, not the public, to pay their salaries.
- Some legionaries were also trained as engineers, surveyors and architects. They designed and built fortifications, roads, bridges and aqueducts.
- Jews were not allowed to join the Roman army.
- A Roman soldier carried his own equipment. In addition to his sword,

A good deal!

Advantages of joining the Roman army

1. *Good pay* – especially for the Imperial Guard.
2. *Bonus* of up to five years' pay for good service.
3. *Retirement bonus* of 13 to 17 years' pay after 20–25 years' service.
4. *Double pay* for soldiers with special duties.
5. *Roman citizenship* – the

Replica of a Roman catapult, for hurling huge stones into a besieged city.

The Romans attack and destroy the Jerusalem Temple in AD 70, during the Jewish Revolt. All that now remains of the Temple is part of the outer wall, known today as the "Western" or "Wailing" Wall.

dagger and shield (rectangular and heavy), he had a 30-kg (60-pound) pack on his back. Heavy supplies were carried in mule carts.

■ Roman soldiers pitched their leather tents in big rectangular camps surrounded by a ditch. They built a stake fence on a high embankment of dirt. The general's tent was always placed in the middle of the camp.

The Roman imperial eagle.

Stone relief of a foot-soldier fighting off a cavalryman.

Bible Nugget

Cornelius was a centurion in the Italian Regiment stationed in Caesarea. God gave Cornelius a vision and told him to send for the apostle Peter. It was God's plan that Peter should tell this Roman soldier all about Christ.

Acts 10:1–7

A Roman centurion on duty.

Medicine

In the earliest days, priests were expected to serve as doctors and help the sick. Later, Jewish men studied medicine under the guidance of priests. The Israelites also learned a lot about medicine from the Egyptians, whose doctors were advanced for their time.

Common skin diseases were leprosy, syphilis, smallpox, boils and scabies. Other diseases included tuberculosis, typhoid fever, malaria and dysentery.

Treatments

Skin diseases – mineral baths and ointments; pastes made from herbs and oils

Boils – a hot fig paste, such as the one applied to King Hezekiah by Isaiah (*2 Kings 20:7*)

Wounds – salt to clean and disinfect; olive oil and wine (*Luke 10:34*); honey

Snake bites and scorpion stings – balm resin

Stomach ailments – wine (*1 Timothy 5:23*)

Other internal diseases – medicines made from roots, pounded into powder; leaves and berries boiled in water

Toothache – garlic

Sore gums – yeast rubbed on the infected area

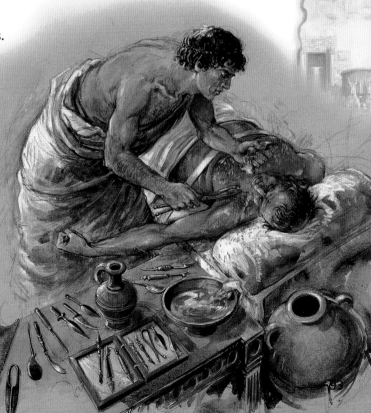

A Roman surgeon at work. Notice his specialist tools.

Jesus heals a crippled man.

The Bible's most famous physician

Luke the gospel-writer. He was probably Paul's personal doctor, and was called the "beloved physician" (*Colossians 4:14*).

Operations commonly performed in New Testament times:

- removal of arrowheads
- amputation
- removal of cataracts (from the eye)
- tracheotomy (making an opening in the throat to help breathing).

Some Roman medical tools:

- *speculum* – to help examine the patient
- *cup* – for bleeding
- *medicine box*
- *hook* – for removing tissue
- *scalpel*
- *spoon* – to warm salves
- *probes*
- *forked instrument* – to remove arrowheads.

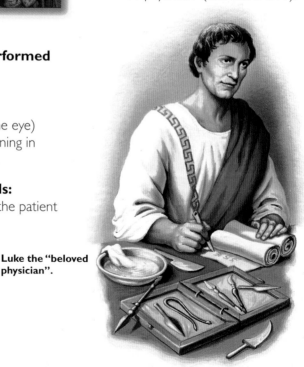

Luke the "beloved physician".

The Tabernacle

Moses with the Ten Commandments.

The Tabernacle was God's home on earth. When Moses received the Ten Commandments on Mount Sinai, God told him to build a special place where sacrifices could be offered (*Exodus 25:8–9*).

The Tabernacle looked like a large tent and was built from materials given by the Jewish people: gold, silver and bronze; blue, purple and scarlet fabric; fine linen; goatskins and hair; rams' skins; acacia wood; lamp oil; spices and incense; onyx and other gems (*Exodus 25:1–7*).

The Tabernacle was portable, like a tent. The Jewish priests took it down and set it up again each time they moved on (*Numbers 9: 15–23*).

A modern replica of the Tabernacle. In the foreground is the altar of sacrifice.

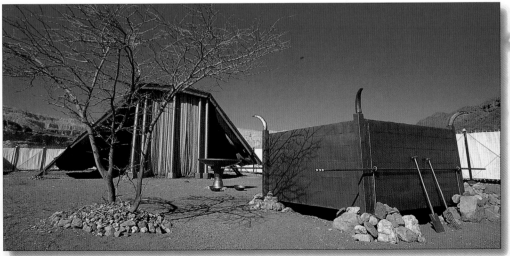

Artist's impression of the Tabernacle. Notice the fence around the central tent. What is burning in front of the Tabernacle? What are the priests doing? Note how the tribes of Israel have pitched their tents all around the Tabernacle.

The Ark of the Covenant was a wooden box covered with gold. Inside were the two stone tablets of the Ten Commandments, a gold jar of manna and Aaron's rod. The Ark was kept in the Holy of Holies where God dwelt, the most sacred place in the Tabernacle (*Exodus 16:34; 1 Kings 8:9*).

Scale model of the Ark of the Covenant.

A special lamp-stand used for the Jewish festival of lights, Hanukkah.

Bible Nugget

When the Tabernacle was built, God occupied this home on earth. The glory of the Lord filled the sanctuary with a cloud. At night, fire was in the cloud. The Israelites broke camp and journeyed on only when God's glory left the Tabernacle and the cloud lifted. *Exodus 40:34–38*

The Jewish high priest in his ceremonial costume.

Sacrifices

In ancient times, the Israelites had to offer sacrifices to God, to gain his forgiveness, to show their love, dedication and faith or simply to give thanks.

Elijah prays for fire from heaven on his sacrifice.

Sacrifices were offered at every religious festival on behalf of all Israelites. During the great festivals, the Temple area was swarming with animals for sale to sacrifice. Pigeons and doves were sold very cheaply (*Leviticus 5:7*).

In animal offerings, blood was sprinkled, splashed, poured or smeared on the altar. Meat not burned was eaten by priests or sometimes by the person making the offering. It was forbidden to eat the fat or drink the blood (*Leviticus 1:11; 7:22–27*).

Some sacrifices were made by a priest, some with the help of a priest and some without (*Genesis 15:9–10*). The altar fire in the Tabernacle – and later the

Temple – was never allowed to go out. Priests added wood continually to keep it burning (*Leviticus 6:8–13*).

Types of sacrifice

- To show devotion to God and be forgiven of general sins you offered bullock, lamb, ram, goat, pigeon or dove as a burnt offering (*Leviticus 1*).
- To give thanks to God you offered oxen, sheep or goat as a fellowship or peace offering (*Leviticus 3*).
- To ask God to forgive sins you had committed by accident you offered

bullock, male or female goat, female lamb, dove or pigeon as a sin offering (*Leviticus 4*).

■ To ask God's forgiveness for sins against him and others you offered a ram or male lamb as a guilt or trespass offering (*Leviticus 5*).

Some rules about sacrifices

1. Every offering had to belong to the person making the offering. You couldn't use your friend's sheep.
2. Every offering had to be given sincerely and reverently. God cared more about the heart of the giver than the sacrifice.

The altar of sacrifice in front of the Tabernacle. What is the priest in the foreground doing?

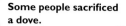
Some people sacrificed a dove.

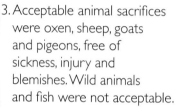

- *Drink offering*: wine poured around the altar, presented with the grain offering.
- *Public offerings*: made in the Tabernacle and Temple on behalf of all Israelites. These included the burnt offerings made daily, on the Sabbath and at special festivals.

3. Acceptable animal sacrifices were oxen, sheep, goats and pigeons, free of sickness, injury and blemishes. Wild animals and fish were not acceptable.
4. Grain or meat offerings included wine, oil and grain. You could not offer ears of grain, meal (coarsely-ground seeds), dough or cakes (*Leviticus 2*).
5. Sacrifices must be either animal (where blood is shed) or vegetable (bloodless).

Samaritans today still make animal sacrifices.

- *Private offerings*: could be made at any time by Israelites, not necessarily in the Temple.

The daily sacrifices

- *Burnt offering*: lamb consumed completely in altar fire, every morning and evening.
- *Grain* (also called *meal*) *offering*: flour or cakes prepared with oil and frankincense; always followed the burnt offering.

Bible Nugget

We no longer make sacrifices because Jesus came to offer himself for us. Now, to be forgiven, all we have to do is ask God.
Hebrews 10:5–10

Music

During the days of Samuel, David and Solomon, Hebrew music was in full swing. Music was very important to the Israelites. Musicians sang or played musical instruments during Temple services, special feasts, weddings and funerals.

Musical instruments of Bible times
Strings

Lyre – With strings made of twisted grass or dried animal intestine, plucked to make a sweet, soft sound. The lyre was the chief instrument in the Temple orchestra. The lyre was played by young David to soothe King Saul (*1 Samuel 16:23*).

Harp – The harp's twelve strings were louder and lower in pitch than the lyre. It was one of the most important instruments in the Temple orchestra. Solomon made harps with imported algum wood (*1 Kings 10:12*). Some harps were decorated with shell, lapis, red limestone and gold.

A lyre-player of biblical times.

103

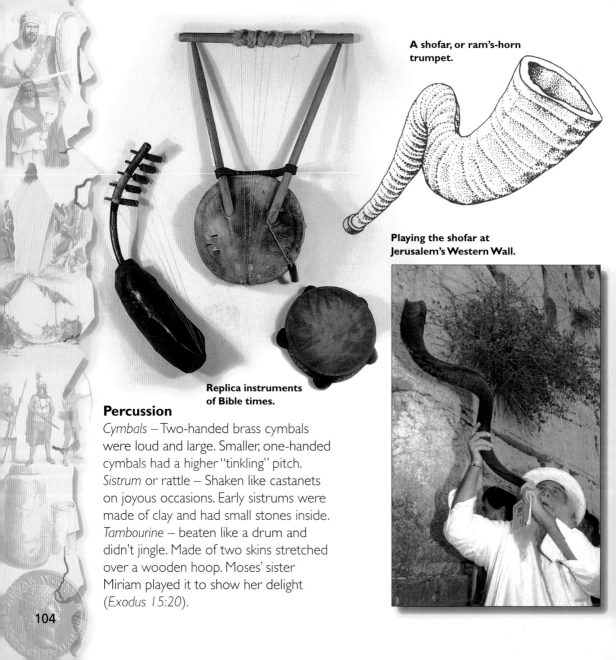

A shofar, or ram's-horn trumpet.

Playing the shofar at Jerusalem's Western Wall.

Replica instruments of Bible times.

Percussion

Cymbals – Two-handed brass cymbals were loud and large. Smaller, one-handed cymbals had a higher "tinkling" pitch.
Sistrum or rattle – Shaken like castanets on joyous occasions. Early sistrums were made of clay and had small stones inside.
Tambourine – beaten like a drum and didn't jingle. Made of two skins stretched over a wooden hoop. Moses' sister Miriam played it to show her delight (*Exodus 15:20*).

Brass

Shofar – A curved trumpet made from a hollow ram's horn. It could give only two or three notes, but was very expressive. Used as a call to worship and to battle. The *shofar* was played during Joshua's siege of Jericho (*Joshua 6:20*).

Trumpet – Straight, long and ending in a bell-shape. In the wilderness, the Israelites were called together by the blast of two silver trumpets (*Numbers 10:1–3*).

Woodwind

Pipe – With two reeds, and probably two pipes, the pipe was made of wood, ivory or bone. It made a wailing sound, but was played at joyous celebrations such as weddings as well as at funerals.

Flute – This was the shepherd's pipe or flute. It was a straight instrument

Joshua, the conqueror of Jericho, with a horn trumpet.

with finger-holes and was played at celebrations and funerals. It was one of the many instruments used by King Nebuchadnezzar to call his people to worship the golden image (*Daniel 3:5*).

Which Bible hero was a mighty warrior, a king and also a gifted musician?
Answer: David! He was a fine musician, wrote and sang psalms and played the lyre for King Saul (*1 Chronicles 23:5*).

Young David playing the lyre.

Solomon formed a large choir for his Temple. It was led by a choir-master, the chief musician. Solomon also wrote more than 1,000 songs (*1 Kings 4:32*).

Bible Nugget

When the ark was brought into Solomon's Temple, musicians played cymbals, harps, lyres and trumpets. Singers raised their voices to God. The glory of the Lord filled the Temple in a thick cloud!
2 Chronicles 5:12–13

The Sabbath

The Sabbath was the Jewish rest day commanded by God (*Exodus 20:8–11*) following his example (*Genesis 2:3*). It was intended to mark out God's people (*Exodus 31:13–17*).

Sabbath dos and don'ts

1. Do use Friday afternoon to finish up your week's work.
2. Women, do your cleaning, refill your lamps, prepare your meals in advance and do your laundry.
3. Don't do any kind of work on the Sabbath. This includes slaves. Cooking, baking, beating with a hammer, lighting a fire, writing two letters, tying certain kinds of knots – even helping injured persons, unless their lives are in danger, are NOT allowed (*Exodus 35:1–3*).
4. Don't forget Friday evening prayer. Three sharp blasts of a ram's horn signal the start of the Sabbath.
5. Do have a special meal with your

The rabbi holds the Torah aloft in his synagogue.

family after the service (prepared the night before). Recite the *Kiddush* – a special blessing said over the wine.
6. Do attend a special service on Saturday morning – more prayer and Scripture readings.

■ Trade was forbidden inside the city on the Sabbath so people weren't tempted to wheel and deal on this holy day (*Nehemiah 13:15–22*).

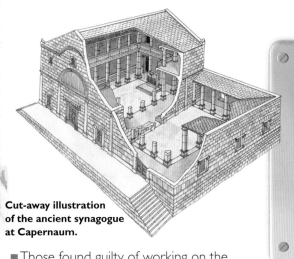

Cut-away illustration of the ancient synagogue at Capernaum.

Bible Nugget

Jesus performed several healings on the Sabbath, to the dismay of the Jews who considered it "work" and therefore unacceptable. He said "the Son of Man is Lord of the Sabbath". On one particular holy day when he healed a paralyzed man, Jesus said, "My Father is always at his work to this very day, and I, too, am working."

Matthew 12:1–14; John 5:1–18

■ Those found guilty of working on the Sabbath were to be put to death (*Numbers 15:32–36*).

Sabbath sabotage

At the beginning of the Maccabean War, in 168 BC, 1,000 Jewish soldiers were killed because they wouldn't defile the Sabbath by defending themselves in combat. Later, they decided that defensive fighting was acceptable. Offensive combat was still not allowed.

In Pompey's efforts to take Jerusalem for Rome, in 63 BC he mounted massive battering rams against the city walls. Since Jews were not permitted to destroy siegeworks on the Sabbath, Pompey chose this day to use his battering rams to break in and take the city.

Sabbath offering

Every Sabbath, priests offered two lambs in addition to a burnt offering. Frankincense and twelve loaves of unleavened bread, representing the twelve tribes of Israel, were also offered (*Leviticus 24:5–9*).

Rabbis carry Torah scrolls in finely embroidered protective bags.

107

Great Jewish Festivals

God told the Israelites to hold a number of special feasts or festivals. These included the Feast of Unleavened Bread, the Feast of Booths, the Feast of Weeks, Passover and the Day of Atonement.

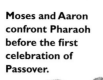

Moses and Aaron confront Pharaoh before the first celebration of Passover.

Jews pray at Jerusalem's holy Western Wall.

A traditional plate containing the symbolic foods eaten at the Passover meal.

Nisan (April) 14	**Feast of Passover**	Very important festival. Celebrates God's rescue of the Jews from Egypt. Eat unleavened bread, wine, bitter herbs and lamb. Retell the Passover story. Thanks and praise to God (Leviticus 23:5).
April 15	**Feast of Unleavened Bread**	Celebrate with Passover Feast. All Jews must attend (Leviticus 23:6).
April 21	**End of Passover**	
Sivan (June) 6	**Feast of Pentecost (or Feast of Weeks)**	First fruits of wheat harvest. Sing, dance and give thanks to God for crops and for giving the Law on Mount Sinai (Leviticus 23:15–22).
Tishri (October) 1–2	**Feast of Trumpets or "Rosh Hashanah"**	Start of Hebrew New Year. Blow horns and trumpets. Read God's Law and feast (Leviticus 23:23–25).
October 10	**Day of Atonement or "Yom Kippur"**	Most solemn day. Ask God to forgive sins of past year. Fast and pray that the new year is a good one (Leviticus 23:26–27).
October 15–21	**Feast of Tabernacles (or Feast of Booths)**	Live in tents to remember how the Jews lived in the wilderness. Offer sacrifices. A week of great joy (Leviticus 23:33–34).
Kislev (December) 25	**Feast of Lights or "Hanukkah"**	Celebrate the rededication of the Temple. Light the menorah candle for eight days.
Adar (March) 14	**Feast of Purim**	Remember Queen Esther saving her people, the Jews. Give food gifts to friends and the needy. Read story in Esther.

A Jewish family celebrates the Feast of Lights, Hanukkah.

The Feast of Tabernacles (or Booths) was to remember the Jewish people's forty years' wandering in the desert. During this festival, Israelite families lived temporarily in tents or shelters, as they did in the desert.

Tabernacles lasted seven days and came at the end of harvest – in fact it was sometimes also known as "Harvest".

The Day of Atonement was the most solemn day in the entire Jewish year. It came just before the Festival of Tabernacles. No one did any work; instead everyone fasted (went without food) and gathered for a meeting.

This fast day was about the washing away of sin. The high priest symbolically transferred the sins of the people to a goat called the "scapegoat". This goat was then released into the desert.

On the Day of Atonement the
high priest released a goat
(scapegoat) into the desert.
This model shows how it may
have looked.

The Day of Atonement, Yom Kippur, is the most solemn day in the Jewish year.

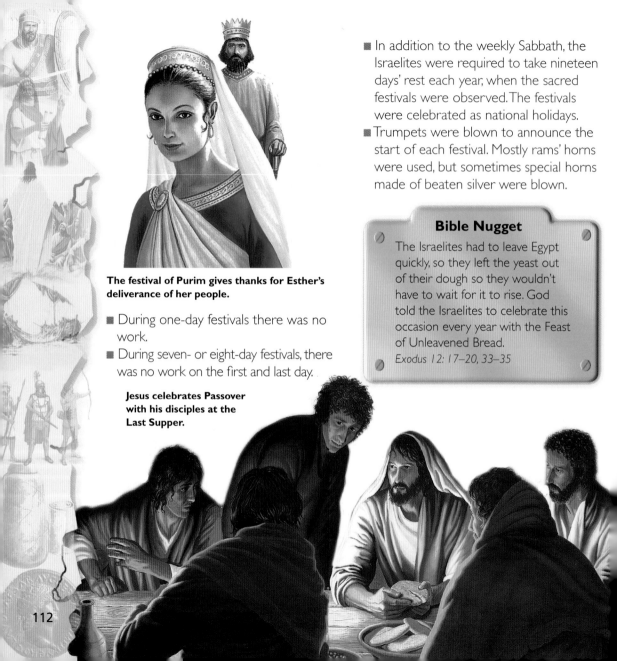

- In addition to the weekly Sabbath, the Israelites were required to take nineteen days' rest each year, when the sacred festivals were observed. The festivals were celebrated as national holidays.
- Trumpets were blown to announce the start of each festival. Mostly rams' horns were used, but sometimes special horns made of beaten silver were blown.

The festival of Purim gives thanks for Esther's deliverance of her people.

- During one-day festivals there was no work.
- During seven- or eight-day festivals, there was no work on the first and last day.

Bible Nugget

The Israelites had to leave Egypt quickly, so they left the yeast out of their dough so they wouldn't have to wait for it to rise. God told the Israelites to celebrate this occasion every year with the Feast of Unleavened Bread.

Exodus 12: 17–20, 33–35

Jesus celebrates Passover with his disciples at the Last Supper.

The Jerusalem Temple

A temple replaced the Tabernacle as the first permanent holy worship place. It stood high on Mount Moriah in Jerusalem and was the chief place of sacrifice.

The young Samuel helps the high priest Eli.

King Solomon's Temple

When David was king, he was upset that God's house was merely a tent. Shouldn't the Lord, our heavenly king, live in a temple that is grander than earthly palaces, he wondered. Although he drew up the plans, David was not allowed to build the Temple. That privilege fell to his son, Solomon, the next king of Israel (*2 Samuel 7:1–5, 12-13*).

In 950 BC, Solomon imported fine materials from around the world and

Artist's impression of Solomon's Temple. The great doors give access to the Holy Place. Further in is the Most Holy Place, sometimes called the "Holy of Holies". Do you know what the great bronze tank in the foreground was for?

113

used expert craftsmen to build the first Temple. There was gold everywhere. People came to worship, offer sacrifices and praise God. But nearly 400 years later, this Temple was destroyed by the Babylonians. Jerusalem was burned and many Jews were forced to live in exile in Babylon. The Temple had been silenced.

A reconstruction of Solomon's Temple.

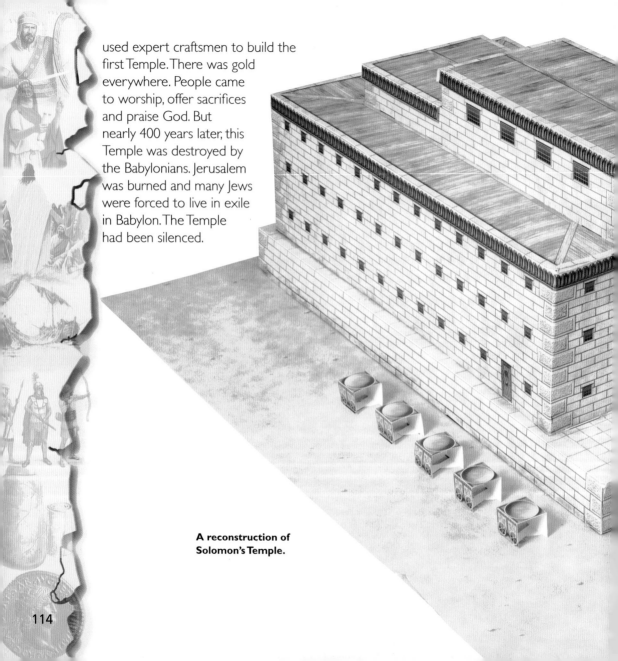

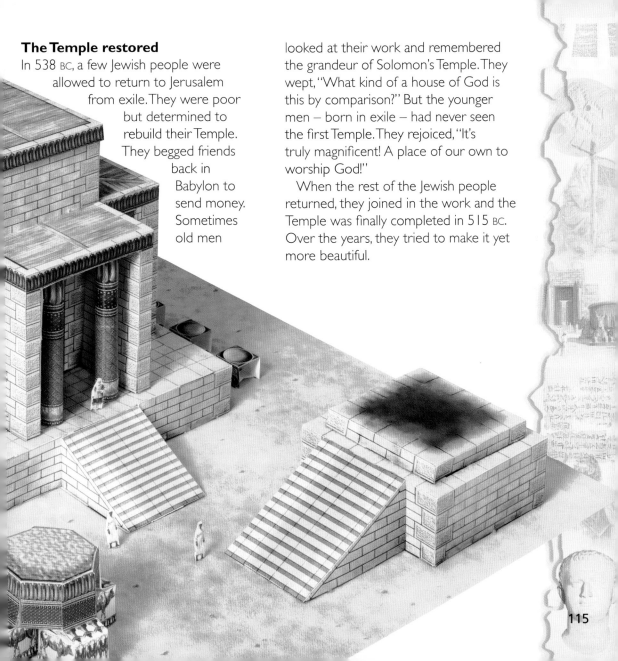

The Temple restored

In 538 BC, a few Jewish people were allowed to return to Jerusalem from exile. They were poor but determined to rebuild their Temple. They begged friends back in Babylon to send money. Sometimes old men looked at their work and remembered the grandeur of Solomon's Temple. They wept, "What kind of a house of God is this by comparison?" But the younger men – born in exile – had never seen the first Temple. They rejoiced, "It's truly magnificent! A place of our own to worship God!"

When the rest of the Jewish people returned, they joined in the work and the Temple was finally completed in 515 BC. Over the years, they tried to make it yet more beautiful.

King Herod's Temple

King Herod the Great had a reputation for making magnificent buildings, and decided to rebuild the Jerusalem Temple. He tried to please the Jews by hiring 1,000 priests, trained as masons and carpenters. The priests worked on the most holy areas of the Temple, which would have been defiled by non-priestly hands.

After forty-six years' work, the white marble structure was completed. Sheets of gold reflected the sun.

Plan of Herod's Temple. The Temple itself is in the middle, surrounded by courtyards. The building upper left is the Roman Antonia Fortress.

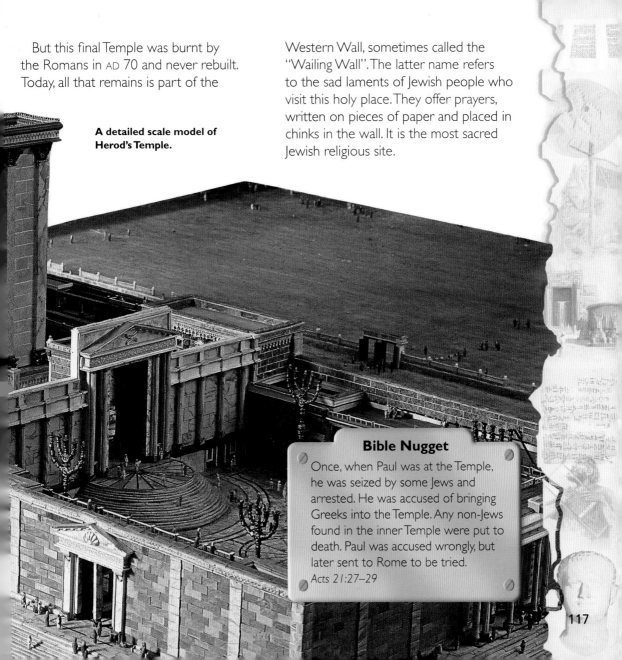

But this final Temple was burnt by the Romans in AD 70 and never rebuilt. Today, all that remains is part of the Western Wall, sometimes called the "Wailing Wall". The latter name refers to the sad laments of Jewish people who visit this holy place. They offer prayers, written on pieces of paper and placed in chinks in the wall. It is the most sacred Jewish religious site.

A detailed scale model of Herod's Temple.

Bible Nugget

Once, when Paul was at the Temple, he was seized by some Jews and arrested. He was accused of bringing Greeks into the Temple. Any non-Jews found in the inner Temple were put to death. Paul was accused wrongly, but later sent to Rome to be tried.
Acts 21:27–29

The Synagogue

The synagogue was not like the Temple. There were no priests and no sacrifices were offered. Jewish people went to the synagogue for several reasons:

- to worship (*Acts 13:14–15*)
- for school
- to study and debate Scripture
- to gather as a community (*Acts 9:2*).

Most towns with ten or more Jewish families had a synagogue. A typical synagogue had many windows, as the Torah was meant to be read in full daylight. Before every service, the floor was rubbed with water and mint.

Inside the synagogue were rows of benches. Men and boys over the age of thirteen sat on one side; women, girls and young boys on the other side, behind a screen. Important men sat in the front row. Everyone faced the speaker's platform.

The Torah (Books of the Law) scrolls

A Jewish man prays in the synagogue. Notice the little boxes tied to his forehead and arm: they contain short extracts from God's Law.

Jesus reads the Torah in the synagogue at Nazareth.

A Torah scroll. It was unrolled from right to left.

119

were stored in an "ark" that sat in a cubby-hole in the side wall that faced Jerusalem. The scrolls were covered in fine linen and brought out after the opening blessings and praises of the service. A member of the congregation was chosen to read the Scripture.

The Torah was read aloud every Sabbath, festival and new moon. It was also read on Mondays and Thursdays (market days). Certain Scripture readings could be read by anyone, even children.

Bible Nugget

Jesus was so well educated in the Jewish tradition that he was called a rabbi. He often taught in the same synagogues he sat in as a boy chanting the Torah.

Matthew 4:23

Remains of the ancient synagogue at Capernaum, built on the site of the synagogue Jesus knew.

School

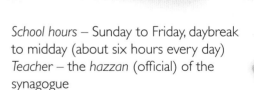

Boys learn the Torah from the hazzan, or synagogue official.

In early times, the Israelites taught children in their homes. They learned to read, write and do basic number work. They also learned by watching their parents and helping them. Schools were started after the exile of the Jews in Babylon.

Elementary school
Bet hasefer ("the house of the book")
Students – boys from five to ten years old
Classroom – the synagogue

A waxed writing tablet.

School hours – Sunday to Friday, daybreak to midday (about six hours every day)
Teacher – the *hazzan* (official) of the synagogue
Desks – wax-covered wooden tablets
Writing instrument – a stylus: pointy side to etch letters in wax, flat side to erase
Subjects – reading, writing and numbers
Textbook – the Torah: the only text ever used

Senior schools
Bet talmud ("the house of learning")
Students – boys ten and upward
Subjects – Students delved deeper into

A young Jewish boy studies the Torah.

Subjects – advanced Scripture studies, writing exercises for future scribes, astronomy, advanced calculating, natural science and geography. Scholars could study further with a "sage" – a great teacher who devoted his life to meditation and teaching. They joined him during prayer, meals and community service, listening and learning as his disciples (*Psalm 119:99*).

The Torah

The Torah was the first five books of the Bible: Genesis, Exodus, Leviticus, Numbers and Deuteronomy. It was the written Law, composed of 613 separate laws, and summed up Jewish beliefs. All education was based around the Torah.

When a master-teacher believed a student could interpret the Law correctly, he was ordained as a scholar – a teacher or rabbi.

the Torah. They analyzed it, discussed it and chanted it aloud to help memorize it. They were asked questions and taught to reason and argue intelligently.

Sometimes teachers held classes outdoors beneath a shady tree. Students gathered at the teacher's feet to chant passages from the Torah or to have discussions.

Bet midrash ("the house of study")

Students – young men eighteen and upward, studying to become a teacher, rabbi or scribe

An ancient Hebrew scroll.

Young Jewish men who wished to become doctors studied with priests who knew the art of ancient medicine.

Craftsmen such as tent-makers and carpenters usually learned their craft from their fathers.

What about girls?

Girls didn't go to school. Their mothers taught them how to be good wives and mothers and how to care for a home, according to what was allowed in the Torah.

They learned:

- which animals were clean and unclean
- how to prepare the food
- how to purify and set the table
- how to purify and decorate the home for the Sabbath and special holidays
- how to spin and weave
- how to treat illnesses with ancient remedies
- how to deliver babies
- how to sing and dance
- how to play an instrument such as the flute, harp or tambourine.

Two Jewish scholars discuss the Torah.

Index